Kim s Last Words, A Cry for Justice

The Untold Story and Profound Bond Between Kim Porter and P. Diddy

Eliza Josh

Copyright

Disclaimer

The content of this work, *"Kim's Lost Words, A Cry for Justice: The Untold Story and Profound Bond Between Kim Porter and P. Diddy,"* is based on publicly available information, interviews, and personal accounts. It is intended for informational and entertainment purposes only. While every effort has been made to ensure accuracy, some details may reflect interpretations or opinions, and should not be taken as definitive fact. The author and publisher do not claim to have access to any private information or relationships and respect the privacy of all individuals mentioned.

Table Of Contents

Introduction

Kim Porter was a woman whose life shimmered with love, glamour, and success, yet carried complexities and untold stories that few truly understood. To the world, she was known as a successful model, actress, and the mother of three of Sean "P. Diddy" Combs' children. But beyond the bright smiles and red-carpet moments, Kim bore emotional burdens, faced personal challenges, and left behind a legacy still being unraveled today.

Her sudden passing in November 2018 sent shockwaves through the entertainment industry, leaving behind unanswered questions and a deep sense of loss. As her death was mourned, a more intricate story began to emerge—one filled with love, heartbreak, resilience, and long-held secrets. Though her relationship with Diddy often dominated the headlines, the true story of her life—her private struggles, her role as a mother, and the legacy she cultivated away from the spotlight—remains largely unknown.

"Kim's Lost Words, A Cry for Justice: The Untold Story and Profound Bond Between Kim Porter and P. Diddy" takes a closer look at Kim Porter's life beyond the media glare. This book uncovers the private moments, hidden truths, and personal challenges she faced throughout her journey. From her humble beginnings in Georgia to her rise in fashion and entertainment,

and her complex relationship with one of the most powerful figures in music, this is Kim's story like never before.

In the years following her death, new revelations have surfaced, exposing layers of her life that were once hidden. The struggles, sacrifices, and secrets Kim carried in the name of love, family, and self-preservation are now coming to light, offering a more complete picture of the woman behind the public persona.

This book is not just a tribute to Kim Porter, but a deep exploration of the emotional and personal complexities that come with living in the public eye. Through her story, we will uncover untold truths, explore recent revelations, and reflect on the powerful legacy she left behind—a legacy that continues to touch the hearts of those who knew her intimately and the public who admired her from afar.

Chapter One

The Early Life of Kim Porter

Kim Porter's life was one of perseverance, ambition, and grace. Her journey began in the quiet town of Columbus, Georgia, and led her to the vibrant worlds of high fashion, television, and ultimately, the heart of one of the biggest names in entertainment. Though many recognized her as the longtime partner of Sean "P. Diddy" Combs, Kim was much more than her relationships. To truly understand her, it's essential to look beyond the glamorous photoshoots and public appearances. Beneath the surface was a woman deeply rooted in her upbringing, a devoted mother who loved her children fiercely, and someone who never lost sight of where she came from.

Born on December 15, 1970, in Columbus, Georgia, Kim was raised in a small city where family and community were central. Growing up in the South instilled in her a sense of humility and strong values that guided her throughout her life. While Columbus wasn't as bustling as cities like Atlanta or New York, it was a place where dreams could be nurtured, and Kim's ambitions were always big. Raised by her mother, Sarah L. Porter, who was her biggest supporter and moral compass, Kim learned the importance of hard work, resilience, and independence—qualities that would serve her well in the unpredictable world she would soon enter.

Even as a child, Kim's striking beauty and natural charisma were evident. Long before she understood the world of modeling and fame, people around her knew she was destined for something greater. Her height, poise, and grace made her stand out, but it was her kind heart and infectious smile that left a lasting impression. Friends recall her optimism, even in difficult times, and a quiet strength that remained with her throughout her life.

At Columbus High School, Kim excelled not only in beauty but also in intelligence and ambition. While she loved her hometown, she knew it was just the beginning. With dreams of seeing the world and a passion for fashion and entertainment, she believed that anything was possible if she worked hard enough.

In 1988, after graduating from high school, Kim made a bold move. At just 17, she left her small town behind and moved to Atlanta to pursue modeling. It was a risky decision, but Kim was fearless in her pursuit of her dreams. Despite the challenges of being a young woman of color in an industry not always welcoming, Kim's determination, charm, and belief in herself set her apart.

Kim's early career in Atlanta started with small gigs—local fashion shows, magazine spreads, and promotional work—but her confidence grew with each opportunity. She didn't just want to model; she wanted to understand the business behind it. Her hard work paid off when she eventually landed a contract with a major New York City agency.

Moving to New York was a pivotal moment for Kim. The fast-paced, competitive city was a world away from Columbus and Atlanta, but Kim thrived. Working with top photographers, walking runways, and appearing in prestigious fashion magazines, Kim's name began to gain recognition. Her work ethic and professionalism set her apart in the fashion world.

New York also introduced her to new circles of friends and rising stars in music, film, and fashion. Among them was Sean Combs, then known as Puff Daddy, an ambitious music producer who would become one of hip-hop's most influential figures. Though their relationship wouldn't develop fully for years, the chemistry between them was undeniable.

Despite her success, Kim never forgot her roots. She stayed close to her family in Georgia and remained grounded despite the whirlwind of the fashion world. Her Southern upbringing gave her the strength to navigate the industry's challenges, and she refused to be just another pretty face, using her platform to inspire young women of color to chase their dreams unapologetically.

As her professional life soared, Kim's personal life evolved. Her relationship with Sean Combs would later become one of the most talked-about in entertainment. But Kim, always independent, took her time to develop their relationship, remaining focused on building her own career.

By the mid-1990s, Sean Combs had become a dominant force in the music industry, and as their relationship grew, Kim and Sean's lives intertwined both professionally and personally. But Kim's story is about more than just her relationship with Diddy. It's about the strength, independence, and determination she displayed throughout her life. She built a legacy on her own terms, inspiring generations to follow in her footsteps.

Chapter Two

Rising to Stardom

Kim Porter's rise to stardom was driven by determination, beauty, and grace. Born on December 15, 1970, in Columbus, Georgia, her early life was far removed from the glamorous world she would later inhabit. Growing up in a small Southern town, Kim was shaped by strong values of family, humility, and hard work—traits that would serve her well in the world of fame. From a young age, she knew she was destined for more. The allure of fashion, music, and stardom called out to her, even though they seemed far from her reality in Georgia.

Her journey truly began in the late 1980s when she made the bold decision to move to Atlanta, a city that was becoming a hub for entertainment and opportunity. It was there that Kim first stepped into the world of modeling, catching the eye of local fashion houses and photographers. With her unique blend of elegance and strength, she quickly stood out. Her beauty was undeniable, and soon, so was her presence in the industry.

However, Atlanta was only a stepping stone. By the early 1990s, Kim had set her sights on New York City, the epicenter of fashion and entertainment. The city's fast-paced, competitive environment was a far cry from the quiet life in Columbus, but Kim thrived. She was determined to carve out her own space, and in New York, she found herself surrounded by endless opportunities. Signed by top modeling agencies, she graced the pages of prestigious magazines like *Elle* and *Vogue*, where her ability to balance fierceness and vulnerability made her a favorite among designers and photographers alike.

Her modeling career flourished as she walked the runways for major fashion shows and worked with some of the most renowned designers. Kim's grace and poise captivated audiences, and her work went beyond the glamour—she was breaking barriers for Black models in an industry long criticized for its lack of diversity.

Modeling was just the beginning. With a hunger for more creative expression, Kim ventured into acting. She knew she had the charisma to succeed on screen, and in 2001, she made her debut in *The Brothers*, a romantic comedy. Although her role was small, her natural screen presence was undeniable, and critics praised her performance. Kim continued to land roles in television, appearing on popular shows like *Law & Order* and *Single Ladies*. She took her craft seriously, always working to improve and grow as an actress.

Despite her success, Kim remained grounded. She valued her privacy and was careful about what she shared with the media, understanding that fame could be fleeting. Her relationship with Sean "P. Diddy" Combs, which thrust her further into the public eye, was often a source of Hollywood gossip. Their love story, filled with highs and lows, was captivating to many, but few truly understood the complexities of their bond. Through it all, Kim remained her own person, refusing to let her relationship define her.

While Kim and Diddy's relationship made headlines, she focused on her own career and built a legacy independent of the public eye. Alongside modeling and acting, she became a successful entrepreneur, launching her own boutique agency and working behind the scenes in fashion and entertainment. Those who worked with her admired her business acumen and determination to succeed in a tough industry, especially as a woman of color.

What truly set Kim apart was her authenticity. She was genuine, warm, and kind—traits that remained constant despite her fame. Friends, family, and colleagues spoke highly of her humility and her willingness to support others, mentoring young models and helping friends navigate the entertainment world.

Ultimately, Kim Porter's journey was about more than just beauty or fame. It was about strength, resilience, and a legacy built on love and determination. She transitioned seamlessly from the world of fashion to acting and business, allowing her creativity and passion to guide her in multiple directions. Though her life was tragically cut short, her legacy lives on through her children and the countless lives she touched.

Kim Porter was more than a star—she was a woman of grace, a force of nature who rose to fame while staying true to herself. Though no longer with us, her untold stories of love, struggle, and success will continue to resonate, ensuring that her legacy endures for years to come.

Chapter Three

A Love Like No Other — Kim and P. Diddy

Kim Porter and Sean "P. Diddy" Combs shared a relationship that captured the public's attention for over a decade, characterized by love, turbulence, and deep emotional connection. Their romance, which began in the early '90s, evolved into one of the most iconic celebrity relationships of its time. But like any love story, theirs was marked by complexities, private struggles, and secrets that only became clear in hindsight. The world saw the glamorous couple that seemed inseparable despite breakups, yet behind the scenes, Kim and Diddy's relationship was far more layered than anyone could have imagined.

Kim, a model and actress, met Diddy at a pivotal point in their careers. Diddy was already making waves in the music industry, managing artists and carving a path toward becoming one of the most influential figures in hip-hop. Kim, with her striking beauty and poised demeanor, had also made a name for herself in modeling. When they crossed paths, there was an undeniable chemistry between them. Their bond was immediate, and they quickly became a fixture in each other's lives.

From the outset, their relationship seemed to embody the classic "opposites attract" dynamic. Kim was known for her grace and calm, while Diddy's persona was one of relentless ambition and energy. Yet, this contrast seemed to draw them closer, as they complemented each other's personalities. Kim was a grounding force for Diddy, who often credited her with being his rock during his rise to fame. Diddy's drive to succeed was unmatched, and Kim's unwavering support allowed him to pursue his ambitions while maintaining a stable home life with her.

However, the demands of Diddy's career and lifestyle soon began to put pressure on their relationship. As his success skyrocketed, so did the attention and temptation that came with being in the public eye. Rumors of infidelity began to circulate, and while Kim remained fiercely loyal, the trust between them began to waver. Diddy, always in the limelight, was surrounded by countless women and partygoers, many of whom sought to be part of his glamorous world. This external pressure weighed heavily on their relationship.

Despite these challenges, Kim and Diddy's love never fully crumbled. Even during the moments when they were apart, there was always a sense of unfinished business between them. Their relationship was characterized by a pattern of breakups and makeups, with both parties unable to stay away from each other for long. Each breakup made headlines, and yet, time and again, they found their way back to one another. This dynamic created a whirlwind of emotions, not just for them but for those who followed their story closely.

At the core of their relationship was a deep connection and mutual understanding. Kim was more than just a partner to Diddy; she was someone who saw beyond the fame and fortune. She knew Sean Combs, the man behind the mogul persona, and her love for him transcended the material world that surrounded them. Diddy, on his part, often spoke of Kim as his true love, the one woman who knew him better than anyone else. In interviews and public statements, he described her as his "soulmate," and despite the ups and downs, there was never any doubt about the depth of his feelings for her.

Their relationship also reflected the complexities of modern love, particularly in the spotlight. For Kim, being with a man like Diddy meant navigating a world filled with constant media scrutiny and public opinion. She had to contend with the gossip columns, the rumors, and the expectations that came with being associated with a man of Diddy's stature. Yet, Kim handled these pressures with grace. She was a fiercely private person who valued her family and personal life above the fame that came with her relationship. Her ability to maintain a sense of normalcy amidst the chaos of the entertainment world was a testament to her strength and resilience.

As their relationship progressed, they became parents to four children, including Quincy, Kim's son from a previous relationship, whom Diddy adopted and loved as his own. Together, they had Christian and twin daughters, D'Lila and Jessie. Parenthood deepened the bond between Kim and Diddy, as they worked together to provide a stable and loving environment for their children. Kim, in particular, was known for her dedication as a mother, always putting her children first and ensuring that they had a strong sense of family despite the public nature of their lives.

However, their relationship continued to face hurdles, and infidelity rumors persisted. For Kim, this was one of the hardest aspects of their relationship. She was well aware of the temptations surrounding Diddy, and while she tried to overlook certain transgressions, the trust between them was often tested. There were moments when Kim chose to step away, seeking distance from the pain caused by the rumors. Yet, even in these moments, Diddy's love for her remained steadfast. He often sought to win her back, making grand gestures and declarations of his love, and Kim, despite everything, often found herself drawn back to him.

One of the most notable public breakups between Kim and Diddy occurred in the mid-2000s when Diddy was linked to other high-profile women. At this point, the relationship seemed irreparable. However, even after this split, the bond between them remained. They continued to co-parent their children and appeared together at public events, always maintaining an air of unity and respect. In many ways, their relationship defied conventional expectations. While they may not have always been together romantically, they were inseparable when it came to their family and their shared history.

The love story between Kim and Diddy was not just one of romance but also of partnership, loyalty, and understanding. They were two people who, despite their differences and the challenges they faced, remained deeply connected. Their relationship was a testament to the idea that love is not always straightforward or easy. It is often messy, complicated, and filled with moments of doubt, but at its core, it is built on a foundation of trust and respect. For Kim and Diddy, this foundation was never fully broken, even during their most difficult times.

Kim's death in 2018 marked the end of their love story in the physical sense, but her presence in Diddy's life has continued to shape him. In the aftermath of her passing, Diddy has spoken openly about the impact Kim had on him, calling her his "best friend" and "the love of his life." He has expressed deep regret over the times he took her for granted and has publicly vowed to honor her memory through his actions and in the way he raises their children.

In the years since her death, more has come to light about the private struggles Kim endured in her relationship with Diddy. Friends and family have shared stories of her quiet suffering, of the emotional toll that Diddy's infidelity took on her, and of her strength in maintaining her dignity throughout it all. Kim, who was often seen as the calm and composed figure in Diddy's chaotic world, carried burdens that few knew about. Yet, she remained steadfast in her love for him and their children.

Chapter Four

The Children They Shared

Kim Porter's role as a mother was undoubtedly one of the most defining aspects of her life. Although her career in the fashion and entertainment industry garnered significant attention, it was her devotion to her children that truly captured the essence of her character. Kim's legacy, which she built alongside her complicated relationship with Sean "P. Diddy" Combs, is perhaps best embodied in the lives of the four children they shared. Each child represented a different chapter in her journey, yet they were all bound by the love and unwavering commitment that Kim had for them.

Kim Porter became a mother for the first time in 1991 when she gave birth to Quincy Brown, her son from her previous relationship with music producer Al B. Sure! Named after the legendary Quincy Jones, Quincy's birth marked the beginning of Kim's journey into motherhood, a role she would fully embrace with grace and dedication. Although her relationship with Al B. Sure! did not last, her bond with Quincy grew stronger over the years. Kim was the primary figure in his life, raising him to understand the complexities of fame, family, and self-identity. As Quincy matured, he pursued a career in music and acting, a path that closely mirrored the artistic ambitions of both his biological father and Sean Combs, who became a father figure to him.

Kim's relationship with Sean Combs began in the mid-1990s, and it was not long before the couple's lives intertwined both personally and professionally. Although their relationship was often tumultuous, one of the constants in Kim's life was her love for their children. In 1998, Kim gave birth to their first child together, Christian Combs. Kim's love for Christian was palpable, and as he grew up, it became evident that he had inherited not just the Combs name but also his parents' undeniable talent and charisma. Christian, known by his stage name "King Combs," followed in his father's footsteps in the music industry, crafting his own identity while paying homage to his parents' legacy.

Despite the challenges Kim faced in her relationship with Sean, including public breakups and media scrutiny, her role as a mother was always her primary focus. Kim had an innate ability to shield her children from the noise and chaos that often accompanied their high-profile lives. She made sure that their family life was grounded in love, stability, and understanding. Her home was a sanctuary where the children could be themselves, free from the pressures of fame and outside judgment. Kim's ability to balance the demands of being a mother while navigating a complicated relationship with Sean spoke to her resilience and inner strength.

In 2006, Kim and Sean welcomed twin daughters, D'Lila Star and Jessie James, further expanding their family. The birth of the twins was a momentous occasion, not just for Kim and Sean but also for the entire family. Kim's joy was immeasurable, and she took immense pride in raising her daughters. The twins quickly became the center of Kim's world, and she dedicated herself to giving them the best upbringing possible. For Kim, motherhood was not just a role—it was her life's calling. She approached parenting with a deep sense of responsibility and care, ensuring that each of her children felt loved, supported, and valued.

Kim's relationship with Sean may have been marked by turbulence, but her co-parenting efforts were nothing short of remarkable. Despite their breakups, Kim and Sean were committed to maintaining a positive and healthy environment for their children. They worked hard to ensure that their personal issues never interfered with the well-being of their family. Kim, in particular, was known for her calm and nurturing presence. She had an unshakeable ability to put her children's needs first, no matter the circumstances. Even when their relationship ended for good in 2007, Kim and Sean remained close, united in their dedication to their children.

Kim's approach to parenting was multifaceted. She instilled in her children the values of hard work, humility, and kindness. Despite their family's immense wealth and fame, Kim made sure that her children understood the importance of staying grounded and grateful for their blessings. She taught them to appreciate the opportunities they had been given while remaining mindful of the responsibilities that came with their privilege. In her eyes, success was not defined by fame or fortune, but by the kind of people her children would grow up to be.

Quincy, Christian, D'Lila, and Jessie were all deeply influenced by their mother's guidance.

They knew her as more than just a glamorous figure in the public eye—they knew her as the woman who braided their hair, helped with homework, and offered words of wisdom during moments of uncertainty. Kim's love for her children was unconditional, and her presence in their lives was a constant source of comfort and reassurance. She was their biggest cheerleader, always encouraging them to chase their dreams while reminding them of the importance of staying true to themselves.

Kim's death in 2018 was a devastating loss, not just for her family, but for everyone who knew her. For her children, it was an especially profound tragedy. They lost not only a mother but a guiding light, a source of strength and wisdom. In the aftermath of her passing, Quincy, Christian, D'Lila, and Jessie have all spoken about the impact Kim had on their lives. They have shared memories of her kindness, her laughter, and her unwavering support. In their own ways, they have honored her legacy, carrying forward the lessons she taught them about love, resilience, and family.

For Sean Combs, Kim's death was also a moment of deep reflection. In the years following her passing, he has publicly expressed his grief and remorse, admitting that he did not always appreciate the depth of their relationship until it was too late. Sean has described Kim as his soulmate, the one person who truly understood him and loved him unconditionally. In his heartfelt tributes to Kim, Sean has often spoken about their shared commitment to their children, acknowledging that Kim's role as a mother was the foundation of their family's strength.

The loss of Kim Porter has left a lasting void in the lives of her children, but her spirit continues to guide them. Quincy, Christian, D'Lila, and Jessie have all found ways to keep their mother's memory alive, whether through their own creative pursuits or by simply embodying the values she instilled in them. Kim's legacy as a mother is perhaps the most profound aspect of her life, and it is a legacy that will continue to shape the lives of her children for years to come.

In reflecting on Kim's role as a mother, it is clear that her love for her children transcended any personal challenges or hardships she faced. She was fiercely protective of them, ensuring that they always felt loved and supported, even in the most difficult times. Kim's ability to navigate the complexities of fame while maintaining a grounded and nurturing family life is a testament to her strength of character and the depth of her love.

Chapter Five

The Secrets Behind Closed Doors

Kim Porter's life was an enigma, wrapped in beauty and framed by fame. She was celebrated for her grace, admired for her motherhood, and deeply loved by those who knew her. Yet behind the glittering exterior was a woman who harbored untold secrets, some of which only emerged after her tragic death on November 15, 2018. These secrets, many of them tied to her longtime on-again, off-again relationship with Sean "P. Diddy" Combs, reveal a story of quiet endurance, sacrifice, and emotional battles that often went unnoticed by the outside world.

Kim Porter and Diddy's relationship spanned decades, with its origins in the early 1990s. They met in 1994 when Kim was working as a model and actress. By then, Diddy was already a rising star in the music industry, but he had not yet reached the pinnacle of success that would come in the following years. Their initial connection was magnetic—Kim was drawn to Diddy's confidence, ambition, and vision, while Diddy was captivated by her beauty, warmth, and intelligence. However, even in the early days of their relationship, there were cracks that would only deepen over time.

One of the biggest secrets Kim carried was the extent of Diddy's infidelity. Their relationship was constantly plagued by rumors of Diddy's affairs with other women, some of whom were famous figures in their own right. In 1999, their relationship faced its first major test when Diddy's affair with singer Jennifer Lopez became public knowledge. At the time, Kim was pregnant with their first child, Christian Combs, born in April 1998. While Diddy's romance with Lopez dominated headlines, Kim remained in the background, quietly dealing with the betrayal. Friends close to Kim would later reveal that this period was one of the most painful in her life. She was heartbroken, but she chose to endure for the sake of her child and the future she still hoped to build with Diddy.

In 2001, after enduring the public spectacle of Diddy's relationship with Jennifer Lopez, Kim decided to leave Diddy, ending their relationship. For a time, it seemed that Kim was determined to move on. She focused on her children, including Quincy Brown, her son from a previous relationship with Al B. Sure!, and Christian. Despite their breakup, Kim and Diddy remained in each other's lives, co-parenting their children and maintaining a close friendship. However, behind the scenes, Kim was still deeply affected by Diddy's actions. While she put on a brave face in public, those close to her knew that she still struggled with feelings of betrayal and sadness over what could have been.

The years that followed were marked by reconciliation and further heartbreak. In 2003, Kim and Diddy rekindled their romance, and their relationship seemed to be back on track. In December 2006, Kim gave birth to their twin daughters, D'Lila Star and Jessie James Combs. For a brief moment, it appeared that they had finally found stability. They were often photographed together at events, appearing to be the picture-perfect family. But behind closed doors, the same issues that had plagued their relationship from the beginning persisted.

Diddy's infidelity remained an open wound. Over the years, numerous women were linked to Diddy, including high-profile figures such as Cassie Ventura, a singer who had been signed to Diddy's record label, Bad Boy Records. While Diddy and Kim never publicly addressed the rumors, it was well-known within their circle that Kim was deeply hurt by his ongoing relationships with other women. In private, Kim confided in friends about the emotional toll it took on her to stay with a man who could not fully commit to her. She felt that Diddy loved her, but his actions often contradicted his words, leaving her feeling isolated and undervalued.

One of the biggest secrets Kim carried was her desire for marriage—a desire that Diddy never seemed willing to fulfill. In interviews, Diddy openly admitted that he wasn't ready for marriage, even though he loved Kim deeply. This refusal to commit was a source of deep pain for Kim. She had invested years into their relationship, had borne three of his children, and had stood by him through countless challenges, yet the traditional commitment of marriage remained elusive. In private, Kim expressed her frustration and hurt over Diddy's reluctance to marry her. She wanted to provide a stable, united front for her children, but she also wanted the validation of being Diddy's wife, not just his partner.

Despite these challenges, Kim and Diddy's bond was undeniable. Even when they were not romantically involved, they shared a deep connection that neither time nor distance could sever. Diddy often referred to Kim as his soulmate, and in many ways, she was. She knew him in ways that no one else did. Kim understood the complexities of Diddy's personality—his ambition, his insecurities, and his need for control. She was his confidante, the person he could turn to when the pressures of fame and success became overwhelming. But being that person came at a cost for Kim. She often found herself sacrificing her own needs and desires to support Diddy's career and lifestyle.

Another hidden struggle Kim faced was the pressure of living in Diddy's shadow. While she had her own career as a model and actress, her identity was often overshadowed by her relationship with Diddy. In public, she was often referred to as "Diddy's girlfriend" or "Diddy's baby mama," labels that diminished her own accomplishments and talents. This was something that bothered Kim deeply, though she rarely spoke about it publicly. She wanted to be recognized for who she was, not just for her association with one of the most powerful men in entertainment.

In 2007, Kim made the difficult decision to leave Diddy once again, this time for good. Their relationship had reached a breaking point, and Kim realized that she could no longer tolerate the emotional rollercoaster that came with being with Diddy. She packed up her children and moved out of the home they shared, determined to create a life for herself and her children outside of Diddy's orbit. This decision was one of the hardest Kim ever made, but it was also one of the most empowering. For the first time in years, she was putting herself and her children first, prioritizing their well-being over her love for Diddy.

Despite the breakup, Kim and Diddy remained close, and they continued to co-parent their children with remarkable grace and mutual respect. Diddy often praised Kim for being an incredible mother, and they were frequently seen together at family events, maintaining a united front for their children. In many ways, their relationship evolved into a deep friendship, one that was built on years of shared experiences, love, and respect. But even as they remained friends, there were still unresolved feelings between them, feelings that Kim carried with her until the end of her life.

Kim's sudden death in November 2018 sent shockwaves through the entertainment world. She was only 47 years old when she passed away from complications related to pneumonia. Her death left Diddy devastated. In the days following her passing, Diddy took to social media to express his grief and regret. In one particularly emotional post, Diddy admitted that he had taken Kim for granted and that he should have married her when he had the chance. His words were a heartbreaking acknowledgment of the love he had always felt for Kim but had never fully expressed.

In the wake of Kim's death, new revelations and rumors began to surface. Some speculated that Kim had been dealing with health issues for some time but had kept them hidden from the public. Others suggested that the stress of her relationship with Diddy had taken a toll on her health over the years. While these rumors have never been confirmed, they speak to the quiet struggles Kim endured throughout her life—struggles that were often overshadowed by the public image of glamour and success.

Kim Porter's life was a complex tapestry of love, pain, sacrifice, and strength. She was a woman who loved deeply, lived boldly, and left behind a legacy that continues to inspire those who knew her. The secrets she carried—the heartbreak of betrayal, the longing for commitment, and the quiet battles she fought behind closed doors—are a testament to her resilience and grace. In the end, Kim's story is not just one of love and loss, but one of a woman who, despite the challenges she faced, remained true to herself and her children, leaving behind a legacy of love and strength that will never be forgotten.

Chapter Six

The Legal Proceedings

Kim Porter's passing on November 15, 2018, sent shockwaves through the entertainment world, leaving behind a legacy that still resonates today. Her sudden death at the age of 47 felt like a devastating blow not just to her family but to an entire industry that had come to know and respect her. Kim was more than just a model or actress; she was a mother, a friend, a partner, and a woman whose presence had a profound impact on those around her.

The news of Kim's death broke quietly at first, with murmurs surfacing in the early hours. But as more information was revealed, it became clear that this was not just another celebrity tragedy. Kim Porter had been found unresponsive in her Los Angeles home, and the cause of death was initially unknown. It left many stunned, particularly those closest to her, who had seen her full of life just days prior. She had reportedly been suffering from flu-like symptoms and possibly pneumonia in the days leading up to her death, but no one expected that this would result in such a heartbreaking outcome.

Sean "Diddy" Combs, the man with whom Kim had shared an on-again, off-again relationship for over a decade, was one of the first to express his anguish publicly. Diddy, who had fathered three of Kim's children, was devastated. Despite their romantic ups and downs, their bond had been undeniable. They shared a deep friendship and co-parented their children with love and respect. Diddy's pain was palpable, and as he expressed his sorrow, it became clear to the world just how much Kim meant to him. In the days following her passing, Diddy posted a series of heartfelt tributes on social media, where he called Kim his "soulmate" and "the love of his life." His words, though simple, carried the weight of immeasurable grief and regret.

Kim Porter's death was ruled as the result of lobar pneumonia after an autopsy was conducted. Pneumonia, a condition that many view as treatable with proper medical care, made the suddenness of her death even more difficult to comprehend. How could someone so vibrant, so seemingly healthy, be taken so quickly by something so unexpected? For her friends, family, and the broader public, the mystery surrounding her passing only deepened the sadness they felt. It wasn't just that she was gone, but the quiet and cruel way in which it happened seemed to rob the world of a woman who had so much more to give.

In the days and weeks that followed, countless tributes poured in from celebrities, friends, and fans alike. Kim's life was remembered for the love she gave to those around her. She was known for being the kind of woman who could light up a room with her smile and her genuine spirit. To those who knew her, she was more than a celebrity; she was a person who made time for others, who was present, and who deeply loved her children. For those who didn't know her personally, Kim was still a figure who inspired admiration, not just for her beauty but for her ability to maintain a graceful presence in an industry often fraught with drama and chaos.

Perhaps one of the most touching aspects of Kim's legacy was the love she had for her children. She and Diddy shared three biological children: Christian, and the twin girls, D'Lila Star and Jessie James. Additionally, Kim had an older son, Quincy, from her previous relationship with singer Al B. Sure. Kim's devotion to her children was unwavering, and she took pride in being a hands-on mother, ensuring that her kids were raised in an environment of love and support despite the complications that came with fame. Diddy, in his tributes, spoke of Kim as not only a wonderful mother but also his best friend, emphasizing how they had raised their children together in harmony, even after their romantic relationship ended. The loss of their mother was particularly heartbreaking for her children, who had always been Kim's priority. In the wake of her passing, Diddy publicly vowed to take on the role of both mother and father, a promise that underscored the depth of their connection.

Kim's funeral, held in her hometown of Columbus, Georgia, was a reflection of the immense impact she had on those around her. The service was attended by many high-profile individuals, including celebrities, close friends, and family members who had shared her journey through life. The outpouring of love and grief was a testament to the lives she had touched. At the funeral, Diddy delivered an emotional eulogy, one that left many in tears. He spoke candidly about the pain of losing Kim and how her spirit would live on through their children. His words struck a chord with everyone in attendance, serving as a reminder that even in death, Kim's presence was still felt profoundly.

But amidst the public displays of grief, there were whispers of untold stories and secrets that began to surface. Kim Porter had lived much of her life in the public eye, but she had also maintained an air of mystery about her personal struggles. While her relationship with Diddy was always a topic of public interest, there were many aspects of their life together that remained hidden from view. Rumors began to circulate that Kim had been dealing with more than just the flu before her death. Some speculated that she had been grappling with deeper health issues, and others hinted at unresolved emotional battles stemming from her years with Diddy. These speculations only added to the aura of sadness surrounding her passing, as the public began to question whether Kim had been silently suffering behind her ever-present smile.

One of the most persistent rumors revolved around the true nature of her relationship with Diddy in the years leading up to her death. While they had parted ways romantically, many believed that their bond was far from over. Some close to the family hinted that Kim and Diddy had been considering rekindling their relationship, while others believed that Kim had come to terms with being a co-parent and a friend rather than a romantic partner. What is undeniable is the profound impact she had on Diddy's life. He has openly admitted in interviews that losing Kim was one of the hardest things he has ever had to endure, and it has changed him in ways he is still coming to terms with.

As the world mourned Kim, her legacy as a mother, a model, an actress, and a friend became clearer. She was a woman who had defied the odds, rising from humble beginnings to become a beloved figure in the entertainment world. Her beauty was undeniable, but it was her spirit that left the lasting impression on those who knew her. Kim Porter's passing left a void in the lives of her children, her family, and the people who loved her. Yet, in her death, she also became a symbol of the fragility of life, a reminder of how quickly things can change, and how important it is to cherish the people we love while they are still with us.

Chapter Seven

The Latest Saga — Unraveling New Secrets

Kim Porter's story continues to captivate the public, and as recent revelations circulate, the complexity of her life, especially her relationship with Sean "P. Diddy" Combs, takes on new layers. Nearly five years after her tragic passing, new information is surfacing about her relationship with Diddy, her personal struggles, and secrets that have only recently come to light.

One of the most prominent headlines circulating right now involves claims about the turbulent dynamics between Kim and Diddy during the final years of her life. Although the couple shared an on-and-off relationship that spanned decades, sources now suggest that Kim had been quietly preparing to distance herself from Diddy before her untimely death. Legal documents from 2018, which recently became public, indicate that Kim had taken steps to secure her financial independence from Diddy, reportedly negotiating property and trust arrangements for her children. This has sparked discussions about the true state of their relationship at the time, adding weight to the theory that, while they maintained a public front, there were deeper rifts behind the scenes.

Another recent bombshell involves the circumstances surrounding Kim's death, which was initially ruled as complications from pneumonia. In 2023, investigative journalists began exploring claims from those close to Kim, suggesting that her death may have been preventable. According to these sources, Kim had been battling health issues for several weeks, and there are now allegations that her condition was not treated with the seriousness it deserved. One friend of the family spoke anonymously to *Page Six* in early 2024, alleging that Kim had expressed concerns about her health but felt overwhelmed by the demands of motherhood and her public life. The resurfacing of these claims has ignited new conversations about the mental and physical strain she may have been under in the months leading up to her death.

Adding fuel to the ongoing saga, a new documentary project has been announced that promises to delve into Kim's life and legacy, including her relationship with Diddy. Directed by Emmy-award-winning filmmaker Ava

DuVernay, the documentary will feature never-before-seen footage of Kim, along with interviews from her close friends and family. Diddy is reportedly involved in the project, though some media outlets have speculated that his participation is an effort to control the narrative around their relationship. The documentary, set for release in late 2024, is expected to bring more secrets to light and could change the public's perception of both Kim and Diddy's relationship.

Most shockingly, rumors are swirling that Kim had confided in a close circle of friends about plans to release a memoir, which would have exposed the full extent of her complicated relationship with Diddy. According to a 2024 exposé by *The Daily Mail*, this memoir would have revealed years of emotional turmoil, stemming from Diddy's infidelities and their turbulent dynamic. The exposé, based on leaked conversations between Kim and a well-known publisher, suggests that she had wanted to set the record straight and share her truth with the world, offering an unfiltered account of her life that was far from the glamorous image often portrayed in the media.

In particular, Kim's experiences with Diddy's high-profile relationships, including his long-term involvement with Cassie Ventura, have resurfaced in media outlets. Throughout their relationship, Kim had dealt with the public humiliation of Diddy's romantic entanglements with other women. In January 2024, a new biography on Cassie revealed additional details about the love triangle between Cassie, Kim, and Diddy. According to this biography, Kim had struggled privately with feelings of betrayal, despite her outward strength and dignity. These new details shed light on just how much Kim had sacrificed emotionally while maintaining her public image.

In addition to the emotional complexities of her relationship with Diddy, the media has also turned its attention to Kim's role as a mother. Recent interviews with Kim's children, Quincy, Christian, and the twins D'Lila and Jessie, have surfaced, offering rare insights into their mother's life. In a candid 2024 interview with *Vogue*, Quincy shared that Kim had been the "rock" of their family, always putting her children's needs before her own, even during the hardest times in her personal life. The children have become increasingly vocal in recent months about their mother's legacy, using social media platforms to celebrate her life and call attention to her contributions beyond her role as Diddy's partner.

The news cycle has also been abuzz with speculation about a recently uncovered letter, reportedly written by Kim just months before her passing. This letter, addressed to Diddy, is said to have expressed her mixed feelings about their relationship. According to *TMZ*'s latest 2024 report, the letter contained a heartfelt message, in which Kim confessed her enduring love for Diddy but also revealed her growing disillusionment with their dynamic. Sources familiar with the letter's contents say that Kim had expressed a desire for independence and had made peace with the idea of moving forward without Diddy in her life. This revelation has added new dimensions to the narrative of their complicated love story.

Beyond her relationship with Diddy, Kim's influence on the fashion and entertainment world continues to be discussed. In 2024, an exclusive feature in *Harper's Bazaar* highlighted Kim's lasting impact as a style icon. Fashion insiders have long praised Kim for her effortless elegance and ability to set trends without trying. The article points out that her influence extends far beyond her association with Diddy, and many are now pushing for more recognition of Kim's contributions to fashion, both as a model and as an influential figure behind the scenes.

While Kim's passing has undoubtedly left a lasting void, the recent surge of interest in her life and legacy serves as a testament to the enduring impact she had on those around her. From her quiet strength as a mother to her public grace amid personal struggles, Kim Porter's story is one that continues to captivate audiences around the world. As more details emerge—whether through new documentaries, biographies, or interviews with those who knew her best—one thing remains clear: the "lost words" of Kim Porter are slowly being uncovered, and her legacy is only growing stronger.

Printed in the USA
CPSIA information can be obtained
at www.ICGtesting.com
LVHW011803291024
795102LV00013B/621